Life in Numbers

The Electoral College

Margaret King

Publishing Credits

Rachelle Cracchiolo, M.S.Ed., *Publisher*
Conni Medina, M.A.Ed., *Managing Editor*
Nika Fabienke, Ed.D., *Series Developer*
June Kikuchi, *Content Director*
Michelle Jovin, M.A., *Associate Editor*
Regina Frank, *Graphic Designer*

TIME is a registered trademark of TIME Inc. Used under license.

Image Credits: inside back cover Joseph Sohm/Shutterstock; p.3 Bizoo N./iStock; pp.6–7, pp.8–9, p.18 (bottom), p.26–27 (all), p.40 Public Domain; pp.10–11 Library of Congress [LC-USZC4-12011]; p.17 Look and Learn/Bridgeman Images; pp.18–19 Frontpage/Shutterstock; p.22 (bottom) Nazlisart/Shutterstock; p.28 Travis Heying/MCT/Newscom; p.29 Newscom; p.30 (bottom) Aquir/Shutterstock; p.31 Jeff Malet Photography/Newscom; p.32 Rex Features via AP Images; p.33 Library of Congress [LC-USZ62-995]; p.34 Tim Evanson (Creative Commons); p.35 Kyle Cassidy (Creative Commons); pp.36–37 Christian Bertrand/Shutterstock; p.39 Bastiaan Slabbers/Zuma Press/Newscom; p.41 Kevin Wolf/AP Images for TV One; all other images from iStock and/or Shutterstock.

Library of Congress Cataloging-in-Publication Data

Names: King, Margaret (Margaret Esther), author.
Title: The Electoral College / Margaret King.
Description: Huntington Beach, California : Teacher Created Materials, 2018.
  | Series: Life in numbers | Includes index. | Audience: Grade 7 to 8.
Identifiers: LCCN 2017055672 (print) | LCCN 2018012704 (ebook) | ISBN
  9781425854898 (e-book) | ISBN 9781425850135 (pbk.)
Subjects: LCSH: Electoral college--United States--Juvenile literature. |
  Presidents--United States--Election--Juvenile literature.
Classification: LCC JK529 (ebook) | LCC JK529 .K56 2018 (print) | DDC
  324.6/3--dc23
LC record available at https://lccn.loc.gov/2017055672

All companies and products mentioned in this book are registered trademarks of their respective owners or developers and are used in this book strictly for editorial purposes; no commercial claim to their use is made by the author or the publisher.

Teacher Created Materials

5301 Oceanus Drive
Huntington Beach, CA 92649-1030
www.tcmpub.com

ISBN 978-1-4258-5013-5

© 2019 Teacher Created Materials, Inc.
Printed in China
Nordica.072018.CA21800712

Table of Contents

polling place

VOTE HERE

A College with No Classes

"Electoral College" sounds like a place you might go to learn about political campaigns, but in this case, "college" means a group of people who meet to select a leader. The Constitution talks about "electors" but does not use the term "Electoral College." A law in 1845 made the name official.

To Pick a President

Every four years, Americans who are at least 18 years old go to **polling places** in November to vote for a president. The candidate who gets the most votes wins, right?

Well, not exactly. On Election Day, people are not directly voting for a presidential candidate. Instead, they are picking a group of **electors** who have agreed to vote for a certain candidate. These electors, chosen across the country, make up the Electoral College. The Electoral College meets in December to elect a president.

One strange thing about this system is that a presidential candidate who gets the most votes on Election Day may still lose the election. This has actually happened in five different elections. Some people defend the Electoral College, but others think it goes against basic ideas of democracy. Why does the United States have this odd system, and how has it affected the nation's history?

THINK LINK

▶ What might be some arguments for keeping or changing the Electoral College?

▶ What might be some other options for electing a president?

▶ What are some pros and cons of having people directly elect their leaders?

Birth of the Electoral College

The idea of the Electoral College began in the summer of 1787. Fifty-five **delegates** from the newly formed United States met in Philadelphia. They would spend a hot summer arguing, debating, and finally agreeing on a new form of government. They set out the rules for this government in the U.S. Constitution.

A New Kind of Leader

The delegates to the Constitutional **Convention** decided on a government with three separate branches—Judicial, Executive, and Legislative (Congress). The 13 states had just won a war for independence from British rule. They did not want a king to order them around anymore. Instead, they agreed on a new kind of leader—an elected president—to guide the nation.

Only in America

No other country elects its top leader the way the United States does. In many democratic countries, the people elect the leader directly. In other countries, lawmakers pick the head of state. But the United States is the only nation where voters choose electors whose only job is to pick the president.

Howard Chandler Christy's *Scene at the Signing of the Constitution of the United States* hangs in the U.S. Capitol building.

Defining the Presidency

The **framers** of the Constitution had many decisions to make about the new nation's leader. They considered having a presidential team, but what if the team members could not get along? Having just one president, instead of a team, seemed like a better idea. They discussed making the president's term two years or seven years before settling on four years.

Big States vs. Small States

As delegates worked to craft the Constitution, delegates from states with smaller populations argued with those from more **populous** states about how to divide power. Should each state have the same number of representatives in Congress? Delegates from large states said that was not fair. Should the number of congressional representatives depend on a state's population? Small states said that would give too much power to big states.

After weeks of debate, delegates finally reached a **compromise** calling for a Congress with two houses. In one house—the House of Representatives—states would elect representatives based on population. In the other house—the Senate—each state would have two members. This plan, called the Great Compromise, would later serve as a model for the Electoral College.

pulation Gap

w large was the gap between big
:es and small states? In 1787, the
gest state was Virginia, with almost
,000 people. The smallest state was
aware, with 60,000 people. Virginia
l more than 10 times as many people
Delaware. Yet under the Great Compromise,
ginia had just four times as many members of Congress.

House of Representatives Chamber during a presidential speech

Growing Body

As the nation has grown, so has Congress. The first Congress met in 1789. There were 26 senators—two for each of the 13 states. There were also 65 members of the House, each representing about 30,000 people. Today, there are 100 senators representing the 50 states. There are also 435 members of the House, each representing about 700,000 people.

Dueling Plans

After agreeing on the Great Compromise, delegates turned to other important questions. One talking point was how Americans would choose their president.

At first, many delegates thought Congress should choose the president. But the three branches of the new government were supposed to be separate. Could presidents picked by Congress act freely? Some delegates worried that they could not. Delegates also worried about upsetting the balance of power between the branches.

Another idea was choosing a president by popular vote—a direct vote of the people. Many delegates believed that ordinary people did not know enough to pick a good leader. Also, because Americans lived far apart and communication was slow, delegates thought that most people would only know about candidates from their own areas. Neither option was perfect.

In Good Hands

Delegates were sure of one thing—the first president would be George Washington. He had led the nation to victory over Great Britain and was leading the Constitutional Convention. Delegates did not want to offend him by debating about how to choose the president. That was one reason they didn't worry about details of the Electoral College system.

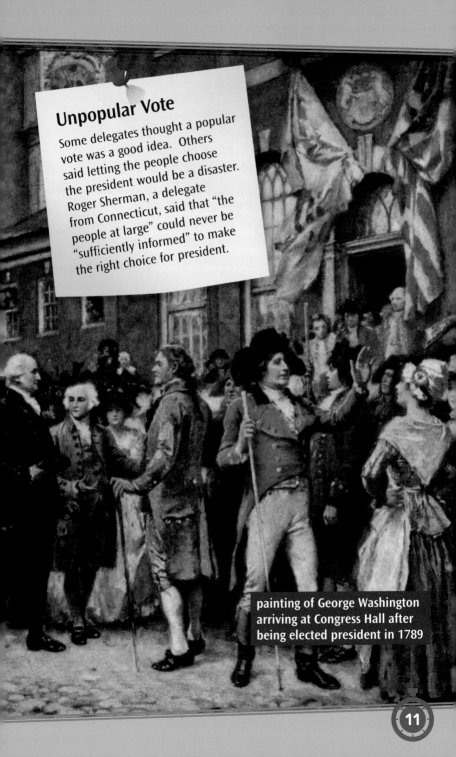

Unpopular Vote

Some delegates thought a popular vote was a good idea. Others said letting the people choose the president would be a disaster. Roger Sherman, a delegate from Connecticut, said that "the people at large" could never be "sufficiently informed" to make the right choice for president.

painting of George Washington arriving at Congress Hall after being elected president in 1789

A Complicated Solution

Delegates were tired after weeks of debate. After going back and forth on the best way to choose a president, they finally sent the issue to a committee to help make a decision.

The committee backed a plan in which states would choose electors who would then select the president. Each state would have as many electors as it had members in Congress under the Great Compromise. Therefore, each state would get electors based on its population, plus two electors based on its two senators. If a majority of electors could not agree on a president, the House of Representatives would decide the winner. In that case, the Senate would choose the vice president.

The delegates quickly agreed on this somewhat complicated system. That's how the Electoral College came to be.

Washington speaks at the
Constitutional Convention.

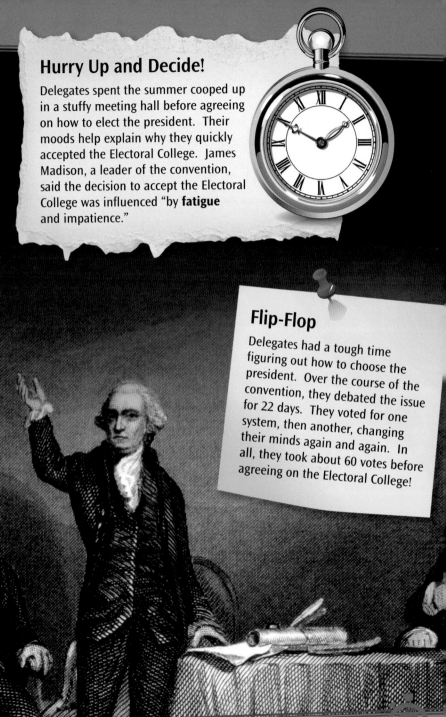

Hurry Up and Decide!

Delegates spent the summer cooped up in a stuffy meeting hall before agreeing on how to elect the president. Their moods help explain why they quickly accepted the Electoral College. James Madison, a leader of the convention, said the decision to accept the Electoral College was influenced "by **fatigue** and impatience."

Flip-Flop

Delegates had a tough time figuring out how to choose the president. Over the course of the convention, they debated the issue for 22 days. They voted for one system, then another, changing their minds again and again. In all, they took about 60 votes before agreeing on the Electoral College!

The Shadow of Slavery

Some historians point to another reason that led delegates to approve the Electoral College—it helped protect slavery. The system gave more power to Southern states with large **enslaved** populations.

As part of the Great Compromise, Southern states wanted to count enslaved people in their population totals. Doing that would give them more members in Congress. Northern delegates said that was not fair, since enslaved people did not have the right to vote. Delegates compromised by agreeing to count each enslaved person as three-fifths of a person.

Since the so-called "Three-Fifths Compromise" gave Southern states more members in Congress, it also gave them more votes in the Electoral College. So, Southern states were quick to support the Electoral College.

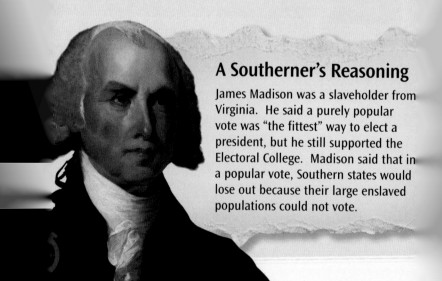

A Southerner's Reasoning

James Madison was a slaveholder from Virginia. He said a purely popular vote was "the fittest" way to elect a president, but he still supported the Electoral College. Madison said that in a popular vote, Southern states would lose out because their large enslaved populations could not vote.

Left Out of Democracy

Enslaved people, who made up about 40 percent of the South's population, were not the only ones left out of voting. When the framers wrote the Constitution, women could not vote, and neither could white men without property. So, a "popular vote" really included just a small part of the population.

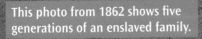

This photo from 1862 shows five generations of an enslaved family.

Fixing a Broken System

The Constitution called for each elector to vote for two candidates. The one with the most electoral votes would be president; second-place would be vice president. In theory, this would make the two most popular candidates the top leaders of the nation. In practice, it caused serious problems.

In 1796, the Electoral College chose John Adams as president. Thomas Jefferson got the second-most votes and became vice president. The two men were from rival political parties, and they refused to work together. In 1800, Jefferson ran for president with Aaron Burr as his vice president. Many electors used their two votes on Jefferson and Burr, so both men received the same number of votes. That sent the election to the House of Representatives, which had to vote 35 times before picking Jefferson as president.

These issues led to the Twelfth **Amendment** to the Constitution. This amendment, **ratified** in 1804, changed the Electoral College. Electors now voted separately for a president and a vice president.

Expected to Fail

Some of the framers thought the Electoral College would fail to agree on a president most of the time. They thought electors would select some good candidates, but in most cases, the House would have to choose a winner. Delegate George Mason predicted that 19 times out of 20, electors would fail to agree on a president. In reality, the choice has gone to the House only twice.

The Rise of Parties

When the framers created the Electoral College, they didn't think about political parties. But powerful parties soon formed. Washington warned that these parties would drive apart "those who ought to be bound together by **fraternal** affection." By the election of 1796, parties were fighting bitterly. That's a big reason the Electoral College needed to be changed.

Th Jefferson   John Adams

How It Works

The U.S. Constitution lets the states decide how to choose their electors. At first, many states let lawmakers pick electors. Over the years, all states switched to letting people vote for their electors.

A Rubber Stamp

The framers thought electors would be citizens who were not tied to political parties and who would cast wise, **unbiased** votes for president. However, as political parties grew more powerful, the Electoral College lost its independent role. Today, political parties hold conventions to nominate candidates for president and vice president. Members of the parties choose loyal followers to be their electors. These electors promise to vote for their party's **nominee**.

The names of electors do not appear on most state **ballots**. Instead, they only list presidential candidates' names. So, to most voters, it looks like they are voting for the president. In actuality, they are selecting electors who have pledged to vote for that candidate.

No Federal Officials Allowed

Who can be an elector? The Constitution doesn't say much on the subject. It does say that an elector cannot be a senator, a representative, or hold "an office of trust or profit under the United States." The framers added that rule to try to make sure the Electoral College would stay independent.

Electoral Math

There are 535 members of Congress—100 senators and 435 representatives. So, there are a total of 535 electors split among the 50 states. The District of Columbia also gets 3 electors, which brings the total to 538. Every 10 years, the U.S. government conducts a new **census**. This updates the population for each state, which adjusts the number of electors for each state, too.

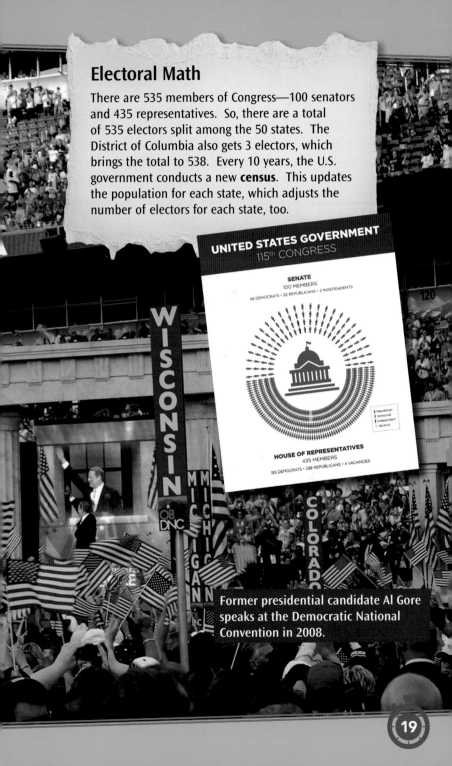

UNITED STATES GOVERNMENT
115ᵗʰ CONGRESS

SENATE
100 MEMBERS
46 DEMOCRATS · 52 REPUBLICANS · 2 INDEPENDENTS

Republican
Democrat
Independent
Vacancy

HOUSE OF REPRESENTATIVES
435 MEMBERS
193 DEMOCRATS · 238 REPUBLICANS · 4 VACANCIES

Former presidential candidate Al Gore speaks at the Democratic National Convention in 2008.

Electors Cast Their Votes

On Election Day, voters across the nation pick a total of 538 electors. In most elections, people know within hours who the new president will be. However, that result is not official. In December, electors meet in their own states to cast their votes. Then, in early January, Congress counts those electoral votes.

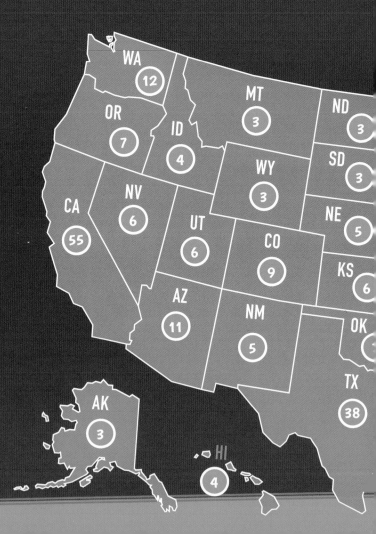

The Constitution lets electors vote as they wish, but most states have laws saying electors must vote for the candidates they promised to support. **Violators** could be punished by having to pay fines. Even in states without such laws, electors almost always vote for their party's nominee.

To win, a candidate needs a majority (at least 270 votes) of the 538 electoral votes. What if two candidates tie or a third candidate gets some votes so no one receives a majority? In that case, the House of Representatives chooses the president from the top three candidates with each state casting one vote.

number of electoral votes per state

Step-by-Step

The system for electing a president through the Electoral College is very complicated! To review how it works, follow the arrows in this diagram.

1 State party leaders nominate a certain number of electors, based on how many members of Congress the state has. These electors promise to vote for their party's candidates for president and vice president.

4 In 48 out of the 50 states, a candidate who wins 51 percent or more of the popular vote gets every single electoral vote for that state. In 2 out of the 50 states, electoral votes for candidates match the percentage of the popular vote that each candidate wins.

51%

5 On the Monday after the second Wednesday in December, electors meet in their own states and cast their votes. In the history of the Electoral College, electors have voted for the candidate they promised to support 99 percent of the time.

2 Every four years, Election Day is held on either the first Tuesday after the first Monday in November or the first Tuesday after November 1 (whichever date comes first).

3 U.S. citizens go to polling places to vote for the president and vice president. Voters are really choosing a group of electors who promise to vote for the candidates being selected.

6 Congress meets on January 6 to count the electoral votes. The nation's current vice president—who is also the president of the Senate—directs the counting of the electoral votes.

7 If no presidential candidate receives a majority, or there is a tie, the House of Representatives chooses the president and the Senate chooses the vice president. If one candidate receives a majority, the outgoing vice president announces the new president and vice president.

Winner Takes All

In the early days, most states split their electoral votes among candidates. For example, someone who won 60 percent of the state's popular vote would get 60 percent of the state's electoral votes. But, as political parties grew stronger, the structure changed. Most states switched to a "winner-take-all system." This means a candidate only needs to win 51 percent or more of a state's popular vote to get all of the state's electoral votes. Party leaders pushed for this system to help their key candidates.

The winner-take-all system allows for candidates to be named president even if they lose the popular vote. For example, imagine one candidate barely wins the popular vote in a few large states. The winner-take-all system gives that candidate all of the electoral votes for those states. The other candidate wins by wide margins in other states. That candidate piles up a lead in the popular vote but falls short in electoral votes.

"An Amendment...Is Justly Called For"

At first, only a few states used the winner-take-all system for electors. But soon, many other states started doing the same. Madison, writing in 1823, said this was a bad system that went against what the framers had in mind. He even called for amending the Constitution to ban winner-take-all rules.

2016 Election Results

Clinton		Trump
232 electoral votes	▼	306 electoral votes
65,853,516 (48.2%) popular votes		62,984,825 (46.1%) popular votes

Other candidates
(5.7%) popular votes

WA
OR
ID
MT
ND
MN
SD
WY
NE
IA
WI
MI
VT NH ME
NY
MA
RI
CT
NJ
NV
UT
CO
KS
IL
IN
OH
PA
DE
DC
MD
CA
AZ
NM
OK
MO
WV
VA
KY
TN
NC
SC
AR
MS AL GA
TX
LA
FL
AK
HI

Exceptions to the Rule

The winner-take-all system is in effect in 48 states and the District of Columbia. The only two states that do not follow this practice are Nebraska and Maine. They split their electoral votes among different candidates.

When the Losers Were the Winners

In five presidential elections, the candidate who lost the popular vote was named president.

Jackson vs. Adams

Tilden vs. Hayes

1824
No majority winner

1876
Winner by one vote

Andrew Jackson beat John Quincy Adams in both the popular vote and the Electoral College. But neither man got a majority of electoral votes. That sent the election to the House of Representatives, where members picked Adams as president.

Samuel Tilden won the popular vote by 250,000 votes. But Rutherford B. Hayes won in the Electoral College by one vote, so Hayes was named president.

Gore vs. Bush

Clinton vs. Trump

1888	**2000**	**2016**
A close call	Ballot trouble	Modern election

Grover Cleveland led in the popular vote by 90,000 votes. But Benjamin Harrison won the electoral vote by 65 votes, so Harrison was named president.

Al Gore got 540,000 more votes than George W. Bush. The Electoral College result hinged on **disputed** ballots in Florida. Gore asked for a recount of the ballots, but the U.S. Supreme Court refused a recount. So, Bush won in the Electoral College by just five votes.

Hillary Clinton received almost 2.9 million more votes than Donald Trump. But Trump won by 74 votes in the electoral vote and was named president.

Case Study: 2016

Let's take a closer look at an election where the loser of the popular vote was named president. In 2016, Democrat Hillary Clinton wound up with nearly 2.9 million more votes than Republican Donald Trump. But Trump won in the Electoral College by 74 votes.

Trump won close races in several populous states, including Florida, Pennsylvania, and Ohio. His margins in the popular vote there were thin. But under the winner-take-all rule, he got all of the electoral votes for those states. Meanwhile, Clinton won by much larger gaps in other populous states, such as New York, Illinois, and California. This gave Clinton a big lead in the popular vote. But she couldn't match the number of electoral votes that Trump earned with his multiple narrow wins.

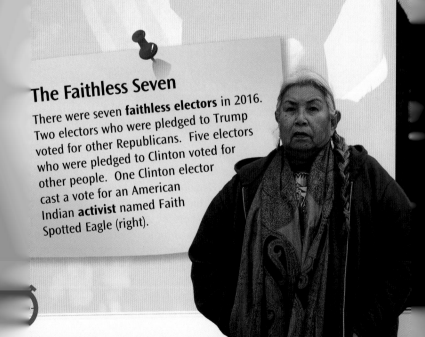

The Faithless Seven

There were seven **faithless electors** in 2016. Two electors who were pledged to Trump voted for other Republicans. Five electors who were pledged to Clinton voted for other people. One Clinton elector cast a vote for an American Indian **activist** named Faith Spotted Eagle (right).

Donald Trump on the campaign trail

Donald J. Trump
@realDonaldTrump
Follow

The electoral college is a disaster for a democracy.

8:45 PM · 6 Nov 2012

153,391 Retweets 112,680 Likes

13K   153K   112K

Donald J. Trump
@realDonaldTrump
Follow

The Electoral College is actually genius in that it brings all states, including the smaller ones, into play. Campaigning is much different!

8:40 AM · 15 Nov 2016

37,599 Retweets 123,487 Likes

18K   39K   123K

Changing Views

Before the 2016 election, Trump was not a fan of the Electoral College. In 2012, he tweeted that it was "a disaster for democracy." Four years later, the Electoral College gave him the win. Then he tweeted, "The Electoral College is actually genius in that it brings all states, including the smaller ones, into play."

Pros and Cons

Many people have argued that the United States should get rid of the Electoral College. But others defend it. Read some of the arguments people have given both in favor of and against the Electoral College.

Arguments in Favor

★ The Electoral College gives a voice to voters in rural areas and smaller states. Even states with **sparse** populations get two electors for their two senators. Instead of focusing just on populous states, candidates must pay attention to voters from all areas.

★ It produces a clear winner when the popular vote is close. For example, in 1960 John F. Kennedy beat Richard Nixon by just 0.2 percent in the popular vote. A recount would have taken weeks. But Kennedy won easily in the Electoral College and was named president.

★ The Electoral College supports a two-party system. To get a majority of electoral votes, candidates must appeal to a wide range of voters. So, the United States has two broad-based parties—the Republicans and the Democrats. Other countries' democracies have a large number of political parties, each with a narrow appeal.

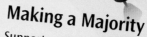

Making a Majority

Supporters of the Electoral Colle[ge]
makes the result clear when no [one]
wins a majority of the popular v[ote.]
Nixon (in 1968) and Bill Clint[on (in]
1992) each won the popular [vote with]
just 43 percent. (That is we[ll short]
of a majority.) But in the E[lectoral]
College, both men had a ma[jority and]
won the presidency.

ELECTORAL COLLEGE
WE NEED YOU

Trouble with Tiebreakers

If electors end up tied, the House of Representatives selects a president. But because each state gets one vote, states with tiny populations have just as much influence as the biggest states. Critics say this tie-breaking system is undemocratic since it gives people in big states less influence than people in small states.

Arguments Against

★ The Electoral College allows a candidate who loses the popular vote to win the election. This makes the Electoral College **undemocratic** since it goes against the basic idea of majority rule. Majority rule is the foundation of a democracy.

★ It goes against the one-person, one-vote idea. States get some of their electoral votes based on the size of their populations. But, because each state also gets two electors representing its two senators, small states get more electoral votes per resident than big states do.

★ The Electoral College **distorts** campaigns by giving candidates a reason to ignore most states. Candidates do not waste their efforts on states where they are sure to win or sure to lose. Instead, they focus on a few key states where the race is close.

Not What the Framers Had in Mind

Supporters argue that the framers had good reasons for creating the Electoral College. But opponents say the system does not work the way the framers thought it would. For example, the framers wanted electors to be independent. But today, political parties choose electors. The electors back their parties' candidates rather than making independent choices.

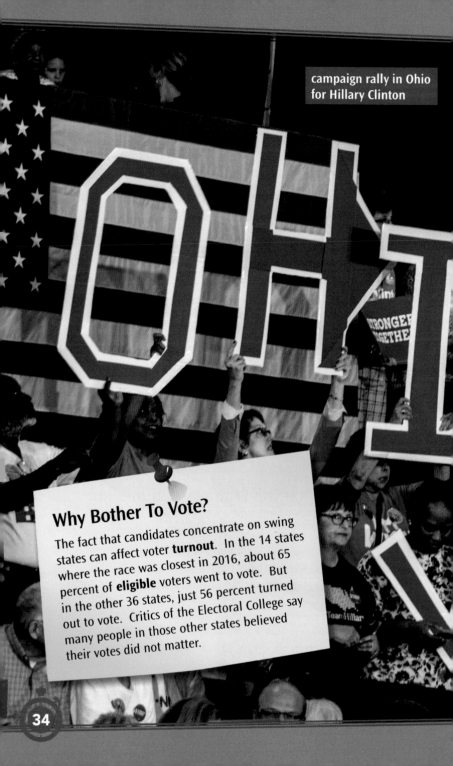

campaign rally in Ohio
for Hillary Clinton

Why Bother To Vote?

The fact that candidates concentrate on swing
states can affect voter **turnout**. In the 14 states
where the race was closest in 2016, about 65
percent of **eligible** voters went to vote. But
in the other 36 states, just 56 percent turned
out to vote. Critics of the Electoral College say
many people in those other states believed
their votes did not matter.

All Eyes on Swing States

One issue people raise with the Electoral College is that it causes candidates to focus on just a few states. Most states strongly support one candidate or the other, so campaigns do not visit those states. Instead, candidates concentrate time and money in a handful of large states where the vote could go either way. These *swing states* usually decide the election.

In 2016, the Trump and Clinton campaigns made dozens of visits to a few relatively large states where the race was close. The most-visited states were Florida, North Carolina, Pennsylvania, and Ohio.

What about the rest of the country? Many other states only got a few visits; 24 states were not visited at all. Even populous California and Texas got just one visit per candidate, since Clinton led comfortably in California and Trump could count on Texas.

Don't Play Favorites

The Constitution says an elector cannot vote for both a presidential candidate and a vice presidential candidate who come from the elector's own state. This rule became an issue in 2000, when George W. Bush and his running mate, Dick Cheney, both lived in Texas. Cheney changed his residence to Wyoming. That allowed electors to vote for both candidates.

Unequal Representation

Another issue with the Electoral College is that it boosts the power of small states. Supporters see this as a plus, but critics view it as a problem. Because of the Great Compromise, each state gets electors based on population plus two extra electors for its senators. The extra electors give small states more representation per person than large states have.

Here is an extreme example of how this works. The state with the fewest people is Wyoming. It has just one elector based on population, but it gets two extra votes for its senators—three electoral votes in all. The state with the most people is California. It has 53 electors based on population. It, too, gets two extra votes for its senators—55 electoral votes in all. Wyoming has one elector for every 142,000 people. California has one elector for every 508,000 people. So, Wyoming has over three and a half times the representation per person that California has!

WY 1 ELECTOR FOR 142,000 PEOPLE

● = 1,000 PEOPLE

CA 1 ELECTOR FOR 508,000 PEOPLE

STOP! THINK...

This chart shows how many people one electoral vote represents in each state. The lower the number, the better representation a person has.

State Name	People Per Electoral Vote	State Name	People Per Electoral Vote
Alabama	405,253	Montana	255,284
Alaska	174,284	Nebraska	273,424
Arizona	433,000	Nevada	339,257
Arkansas	367,407	New Hampshire	257,309
California	508,344	New Jersey	480,477
Colorado	422,621	New Mexico	308,101
Connecticut	393,869	New York	519,075
Delaware	230,723	North Carolina	483,590
Florida	510,318	North Dakota	174,240
Georgia	449,756	Ohio	489,209
Hawaii	264,121	Oklahoma	403,098
Idaho	284,628	Oregon	423,517
Illinois	485,073	Pennsylvania	495,511
Indiana	443,228	Rhode Island	207,153
Iowa	386,394	South Carolina	393,877
Kansas	354,363	South Dakota	203,794
Kentucky	414,500	Tennessee	440,919
Louisiana	426,920	Texas	481,046
Maine	263,457	Utah	315,476
Maryland	442,059	Vermont	165,503
Massachusetts	446,246	Virginia	472,873
Michigan	471,223	Washington	428,599
Minnesota	401,986	West Virginia	293,115
Mississippi	368,624	Wisconsin	434,749
Missouri	456,349	Wyoming	142,741

Source: 2010 United States Census

》 Which three states have the most people for each electoral vote? Which three states have the fewest people for each electoral vote?

》 Is this way of representation democratic? Why or why not?

A Stubborn System

A lot of people have problems with the Electoral College. Polls show that less than half of Americans support it. Over the years, people have proposed more than seven hundred constitutional amendments to change the Electoral College. That's more than on any other subject. There were new requests for change in 2016 after Trump won the election while losing the popular vote.

Some people want to eliminate the Electoral College and choose a president by popular vote. Others want to change parts of the system, such as getting rid of winner-take-all rules.

However, many experts think it is unlikely that the Electoral College will end any time soon. For one thing, amending the Constitution is difficult. And states that benefit from the Electoral College will most likely vote to keep it.

t in Stone

framers purposely made it hard to change
Constitution. Proposing an amendment
ures a two-thirds vote in both houses of
gress. Then, three-fourths of the states
t agree. Another way to amend the
stitution is by having two-thirds of state
slatures request a national convention.
this method is even more difficult.

People ask the Electoral College to vote against Trump in 2016.

No Amendment Needed

The National Popular Vote Interstate Compact wants to change the Electoral College without amending the Constitution. Under this plan, states agree to give all their electoral votes to the winner of the national popular vote. So far, 11 states have joined. But the new system will take effect only if it wins support from enough states to make up an Electoral College majority—270.

What Do You Think?

The Electoral College is a complex system that grew out of the United States' rich history. Some of the ideas behind the Electoral College—such as making sure smaller states were given a voice—still apply today. However, the Electoral College has changed over the years in ways that the framers of the Constitution did not **anticipate**.

Based on what you have learned, do you believe the Electoral College is the best option the United States has to elect a president? Think about the advantages and disadvantages of the system. Does one side outweigh the other in your opinion? Learning about the strengths and weaknesses of the system enables you to form a well-grounded opinion. It lets you speak your mind freely, which is the true basis of a democracy.

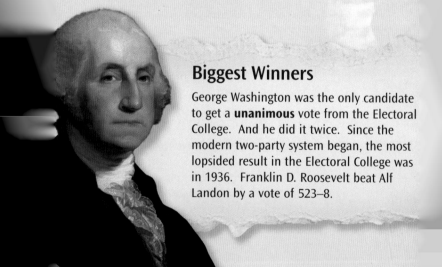

Biggest Winners

George Washington was the only candidate to get a **unanimous** vote from the Electoral College. And he did it twice. Since the modern two-party system began, the most lopsided result in the Electoral College was in 1936. Franklin D. Roosevelt beat Alf Landon by a vote of 523–8.

Color-Coded States

On election night in 1976, NBC News displayed a map using red for states won by Democrat Jimmy Carter and blue for states won by Republican Gerald Ford. Other news programs began using similar maps, sometimes switching the colors. Over time, they agreed to use red for Republican states and blue for Democratic states. Those colors are still used today.

NewsOne Now's host Roland S. Martin checks the 2016 Electoral Map during a live broadcast.

Glossary

activist—a person who uses strong actions to try to make changes in society

amendment—a change in the words or meaning of a document, such as the Constitution

anticipate—to foresee or deal with in advance

ballots—tickets or pieces of paper used to vote in elections

census—a complete count of the population

compromise—a way to reach an agreement in which each side gives something up

convention—a large meeting of people who work together to make decisions for a group

delegates—people who are elected or chosen to vote or act for others

disputed—disagreed upon

distorts—changes the natural shape or appearance of something in a negative way

electors—members of the Electoral College who have the right to vote in an election

eligible—able to do or receive something

enslaved—held in a state of slavery

faithless electors—members of the Electoral College who vote for different presidential candidates than the ones they have pledged to vote for

fatigue—a state of extreme tiredness

framers—the people who wrote the U.S. Constitution

fraternal—friendly or brotherly

nominee—someone who has been chosen as a candidate for a job or position

polling places—where people vote during elections

populous—having a large population

ratified—made official by signing or approving

sparse—small in number or amount

turnout—the number of people who participate in something

unanimous—agreed to by everyone

unbiased—not showing or having an unfair tendency to believe or support some people or ideas over others

undemocratic—not agreeing with democratic practices or ideas

violators—those who do things that are not allowed

Index

Check It Out!

Books

Edwards, George C., III. 2011. *Why the Electoral College Is Bad for America, 2nd Edition.* New Haven, CT: Yale University Press.

Monk, Linda R. 2015. *The Words We Live By: Your Annotated Guide to the Constitution.* New York: Stonesong Press Books.

Ross, Tara. 2016. *We Elect a President: The Story of Our Electoral College.* Ashland, OH: Colonial Press.

Videos

Ted Ed. 2012. *Does Your Vote Count? The Electoral College Explained – Christina Greer.*

Websites

270towin.com. *Presidential Election Map.* www.270towin.com.

PBS Learning Media. *Election Central.* www.pbseduelectioncentral.com/.

National Archives and Records Administration. *U.S. Electoral College Historic Election* Results. www.archives.gov/federal-register/electoral-college/map/historic.html#2012.

Try It!

People have strong opinions about the Electoral College. Now that you have an understanding of the subject, create a video that will convince people to agree with your side of the argument.

- ✔ Divide a sheet of paper into two columns. Label the left column *video* and the right column *audio*.

- ✔ In the *audio* column, write the script for your video. Be sure to explain clearly how the Electoral College works, and include arguments for and against your stance on the system. Make note of any other sounds which you plan to include, such as music or interviews, in the *audio* column as well.

- ✔ In the *video* column, describe what will appear on-screen to accompany each part of your script. This will probably include shots of you talking, as well as photographs, diagrams, or maps to illustrate different aspects of the Electoral College.

- ✔ If possible, record your video using a camera or smartphone. Show it to classmates who have different opinions than you, and ask them whether it persuaded them to change their stances.

About the Author

Margaret King grew up in San Diego County, California. She graduated from the University of California, Berkeley, with a degree in history and English. She also has a master's degree in journalism from Columbia University. King worked at a daily newspaper in a variety of editing positions, including politics editor. Later, she was a writer for Sally Ride Science, a company started by the first American woman in space. King and her husband live in San Diego. They have three grown children.